"Caring for another person is one of life's greatest challenges, one that daily threatens our sense of peace. But, as Mary Tutterow reminds us in *The Peaceful Caregiver*, caregiving is also a divine assignment from God. And God promises that His peace is possible no matter our circumstances. In *The Peaceful Caregiver*, Mary shares practical biblical advice to help caregivers choose the peace God offers. She walks readers through five ways to practice peace and shows us from Scripture how to foster peace with God, ourselves, and others. This great resource can be used by individuals or in groups."

—Kathy Howard, New Hope author and fellow caregiver

"*The Peaceful Caregiver* guides the reader to a place of solace, a tough chore considering the rigorous curriculum of caregiving. Mary Tutterow offers the reader an adventure of the head, heart, and soul on the way to harmony. Scores of Scripture passages in the book offer abundant opportunities for slowing, quieting, reflecting, journaling, and sharing. Mary is a guide helping family caregivers be intentional and tactical on our path to a more peace-filled experience. Family caregiving can be a gratifying, enriching experience. *The Peaceful Caregiver* guides the reader on an intentional journey toward meaning, fulfillment, and a more profound sense of one's calling to be a family caregiver."

—Warren Hébert, DNP, RN, CAE, FAAN, RWJF Executive
Nurse Fellow 06–09, Chief Executive Office

"A lot of how-to books have been written about caregiving. But as a long-time caregiver, I can say with certainty that it's our relationships—with doctors, friends, and others going through the same kind of things—that help us make it through the tough times. And the most important relationship is the one we have with Jesus Christ. *The Peaceful Caregiver* isn't a how-to caregiver book. It's a how-to-find-peace-with-God caregiving book."

—Kathy Harris, author of the Christian novel *Deadly Commitment* and fellow caregiver

"Mary Tutterow brings enormous credibility and experience to address the frenetic heart of family caregivers. In *The Peaceful Caregiver* she gently leads fellow caregivers on a path she herself continues to walk—a path of trusting God with harsh realities. Clearly communicating God's reassuring hand on our shoulders as we care for others, Mary helps us discover a deeper relationship with God in the midst of our journey as caregivers."

—Peter Rosenberger, caregiver for more than thirty years, author, and host of *Hope for the Caregiver*

"*The Peaceful Caregiver* is definitely a must-read study guide for anyone traveling the caregiver journey. If anyone can shed light, love, and blessing upon your personal caregiver journey, it truly is Mary Tutterow. Her books truly embrace and empower you as well as let you know you are not alone. Mary continues to travel her lifelong journey as a caregiver, and she speaks our language as caregivers. I have had the privilege and honor of not only reading her books but also of meeting and interviewing her in person. She is heaven sent and has developed these tools for us. As the saying goes, 'Just because I carry it all so well doesn't mean it's not heavy.' She gets it, and, my follow caregivers, you are not alone."

—Tammy Flynn, mother, caregiver, and producer of *The On-Air Advocate*

THE PEACEFUL

CAREGIVER

From Stressed to Blessed

MARY TUTTEROW

ASCENDER
BOOKS
An Imprint of Iron Stream Media

Birmingham, Alabama

Other Ascender Books by Mary Tutterow
The Heart of the Caregiver: From Overwhelmed to Overjoyed

Ascender Books
An imprint of Iron Stream Media
100 Missionary Ridge
Birmingham, AL 35242
IronStreamMedia.com

Library of Congress Cataloging-in-Publication Data

Names: Tutterow, Mary, 1960- author.
Title: The peaceful caregiver : from stressed to blessed / Mary Tutterow.
Description: Birmingham : Ascender Books, 2019.
Identifiers: LCCN 2019036171 (print) | LCCN 2019036172 (ebook) | ISBN 9781563092954 (trade paperback) | ISBN 9781563092978 (epub)
Subjects: LCSH: Caregivers—Religious life. | Peace of mind—Religious aspects—Christianity.
Classification: LCC BV4910.9 .T88 2019 (print) | LCC BV4910.9 (ebook) | DDC 248.8/6—dc23
LC record available at https://lccn.loc.gov/2019036171
LC ebook record available at https://lccn.loc.gov/2019036172

ISBN-13: 978-1-56309-295-4
Ebook ISBN: 978-1-56309-297-8

1 2 3 4 5—23 22 21 20 19

For Mary Addison

CONTENTS

ACKNOWLEDGMENTS

If it hadn't been for the grace and wisdom of God, I would not be married to my best friend. Because he is my best friend, our relationship has made it through some very tough times. But because my husband has, and always has had, a servant's heart, he's humbly and patiently walked our family through incredibly difficult lessons. We've fought along the way, but a servant leader gets the group where they need to go every time. Winn, I love you and am grateful to God for putting us together so many years ago.

And then there's my posse to thank, those very special people who have come to my small groups and retreats and ended up teaching me more than I ever taught them. Thank you, Mel, Nancy, Donna, Sister Donna, Joy, Shelia, Rose, Fran, Val, and so many more. Beyond friends. My teachers.

THE HEART OF THE CAREGIVER MINISTRY

The Heart of the Caregiver is a ministry for caregivers of all kinds and all generations, whether you're caring for a parent, partner, spouse, sibling, child, or other loved one. You can receive immediate comfort and relief from the pages of this study guide. Some will want to go deeper and connect with others through our live online groups. You may even be inspired to start and lead groups in your church or community.

Visit www.TheHeartoftheCaregiver.com and sign up for free insight and inspiration to your inbox! You'll also receive notifications of retreats, online workshops, webinars, and podcasts, as well as upcoming information on follow-up courses and very special gifts for caregivers!

You are invited to join the closed group on Facebook (www.facebook.com /groups/theheartofthecaregiver), where you can meet other caregivers from around the world and share your needs and thoughts.

You're not alone!

The Heart of the Caregiver ministry is also a tool in the hands of the church to address the caregiving crisis. We believe that by learning to love and care for ourselves first as beloved children of God, we can offer better care to others and offer a kingdom solution to a worldwide crisis.

We also know that those doing the heavy lifting of caregiving can find it nearly impossible to get to church. We encourage direct-to-family ministry, reaching out to meet families where they are with materials and programs to get them reconnected to God's Word and community.

Learn more about the materials and programs available for your church at www.TheHeartoftheCaregiver.com or TheHeartoftheCaregiver@gmail.com.

FROM STRESSED TO BLESSED

Every word in this book was written for you. It was written with love and complete understanding of how hard it can be to take care of someone—even someone you love dearly. It was written so you could experience the life-changing transformation my own family has undergone—from stressed to blessed.

It's been a process, but I am finally in a place where I feel I can tell you that I've made it. *We've* made it. My family's caregiving days are far from over, but my husband and I, even our son, have gone from living lives of constant stress, fear, threat, angst, and guilt to living the peace and joy promised in Christ. It's a daily walk, but with the principles we've learned and shared in this book, we walk in peace.

This study guide is my attempt to walk you in nine chapters through our twenty-seven years of learning from Him. We've not only walked it, but we've been teaching it along the way to see what resonated with people—all kinds of people. We've shared with men and women, parents and children, husbands and wives. These messages are not mine. They are messages from Scripture anointed to help us return to the beautiful and essential art of taking care of each other.

The Peaceful Caregiver is not only a map to help you, a family caregiver, learn to love and care for yourself and others well, but it is also a call to the entire church, the blessed company of *all* faithful people, to awaken to who we are in Christ and why we are here—to love our neighbor as ourselves.

As we as believers realize whose we are and why we are here and the freedom we have to not listen and react to the lies of this world, chains have fallen off. Joy has returned. We are experiencing new life like we never knew existed. We enjoy intimacy with our Holy and Living God.

In the kingdom of God, there is no greater love than to lay down your life for another. If He has called you to that, consider yourself highly favored, and prepare for all the good He has planned for you.

By simply choosing to do this study, whether on your own or with others, you have taken two huge steps toward transformation.

First you've chosen to take time out from your caregiving responsibilities to do something for yourself. That's often the most difficult step of all. Finding a way to make time to do this probably took a lot of effort, but you'll soon begin to see the rich rewards for your efforts.

Second you've chosen to seek out God's Truth about your situation. There are a lot of support groups, self-help books, and friendly advice out there, but if you are seeking true transformation, a new way to live and love—only God's Word and the indwelling of His Holy Spirit have the power to transform.

The Heart of the Caregiver study series is designed to offer support, resources, and community to caregivers through study materials, videos, online courses, a website, newsletter, and more.

You can benefit from the study guide on your own, but I strongly encourage you to connect to community—in online groups or in local groups. The intent is to help you learn God's Truth about yourself, your situation, and the person you care for, as well as to connect you with others who will help you understand that you're not alone in your situation or feelings.

Since the days of the early church, God has inspired and encouraged people to gather in small groups to share with one another about what God is doing and to lean on each other for support and encouragement.

> *And let us consider how we may spur one another on toward love and good deeds, not giving up meeting together, as some are in the habit of doing, but encourage one another—and all the more as you see the Day approaching.*
>
> —*HEBREWS 10:24–25*

> *Therefore encourage one another and build each other up, just as in fact you are doing.*
>
> —*1 THESSALONIANS 5:11*

By attending small group sessions (either in person or online), you will:

1. Discover that you are not the only one who struggles.
2. Learn new approaches to healthy self-care while improving the quality of care you provide for others.
3. Enjoy support and encouragement from others who can laugh and cry with you.

The Heart of the Caregiver logo represents the love that will blossom when God's heart, your heart, the heart of the person you care for, and the heart of community connect. Together can we can bear and even overcome suffering (represented by the cross in the center).

GROUP LEADER'S GUIDE

Author's Note

Thank you for stepping up to lead a group of caregivers in your community! As you may know, people who are caring for a loved one often end up overwhelmed, exhausted and isolated. Too often our caregiving duties have separated us from normal activities/routine—that includes time in God's Word and fellowship.

Getting caregivers connected, talking, sharing, even laughing, can break through the negative emotions and habits that form when we're alone with and afraid of suffering.

Leadership

There are many different leadership styles, and any of them can work with *The Peaceful Caregiver* study guide. A good leader is transparent, ready to share, ready to encourage, and committed to keeping things moving forward.

A simple approach is a book club format. The group is assigned a chapter a week and then you discuss it together.

Some leaders choose to open and close in prayer as well as make time to pray for member concerns.

Some leaders have members read the Scripture in the workbook out loud. Some go even further by doing additional Scripture research to add to the study.

Group Focus

Unlike a typical support group, the focus of The Heart of the Caregiver groups is the emotional and spiritual transformation of the caregivers. These groups are not about the disease or disability but about the ever-present and powerful support of God to do the loving, caring, and healing through us. While each person will need to share their specific and unique situation, the leader's primary goal is to keep the group focused on what God's Word has to say about loving and caring for others.

Gathering the Group

The content is meant to apply to caregivers of all kinds—for instance parents of children with exceptional needs, adult children caring for parents with Alzheimer's or dementia, or a person caring for their spouse with cancer. The content works for men and women, young and old. The groups can be specific (only for moms of small children with special needs) or they can have broad reach (anyone who is a caregiver). The content and discussions are beneficial to all.

You may want to only open your group to people in your faith community, or you may choose to send an open invitation to the broader community through word of mouth or advertising.

There is no perfect size for the group, but for a first time, six to eight members is manageable.

The best time of day to offer a group is when caregivers have other means of support. That may be during the morning when day programs and respite care are available. Lunchtime is also good when people can bring their bagged lunch. Evenings tend to be more difficult due to supper, bath time, homework, and lack of availability of respite workers.

If you're having a hard time finding space at a suitable hour, you may want to consider hosting an online group through free and simple-to-use video chat services.

Setting

There are many different settings that work for this kind of small group. The Heart of the Caregiver groups have been held in private homes, church halls, community centers, in video chat rooms online, and even the chapel of a hospital! There is no right or wrong setting. However there are things you can do to make the group more comfortable to share with each other.

- Always have a box of tissues on hand. People need to know it's okay to cry.
- In the first few sessions, have name tags for people to wear until names are familiar.
- Take a roster collecting email and phone numbers. If there is a reason the group session needs to be moved or canceled, you can easily communicate. Groups also tend to bond and want to contact each other. Ask members if they are okay sharing contact information among members.

First Session

The first session is meant to be an icebreaker. Ask each member to briefly share their name and the relationship and condition of the person they are caring for (i.e. my daughter with special needs, my husband with Alzheimer's, etc.).

It's important to have a group discussion about all the things that are keeping participants from peace. Knowing others are struggling with similar issues, thoughts, and feelings is bonding and provides immediate relief for those who thought they were the only ones struggling. This exercise alone may take the whole hour, but it's very important.

Length of the Course

There are nine chapters in *The Peaceful Caregiver*. However that does not mean there have to be nine sessions. Usually the course is offered as a ten-week commitment, but allow your group to help you determine if they want to go faster or slower. If you're experiencing rich participation and bonding, you may want to vote on spending more time on the study. As a matter of fact, most caregivers find it difficult for the group to end. Many do the study more than once. Some groups go on to find new material to discuss while staying together.

Advice

We're all on a journey, but the destination is different for each one of us. Only God knows the point of our struggles. Somehow He's working it all together for good. The small group is a safe place where we can express and share and experience relief. It is a place of grace, mercy and understanding.

We cannot fix each other; only God can do that. There's great power in allowing what is to just be. When we allow—rather than try to fix, control, worry about, or change something—we leave room for God to work things out His perfect way: the way that's right for everyone involved.

A small group is a safe place to share and learn from others. To keep the time productive and fulfilling, here are a few simple guidelines that should be read at the beginning of each session.

Small Group Guidelines

1. We will begin and end on time out of respect for each other.
2. Everything that is shared in the group stays in the group unless a member has threatened to harm themselves or others.

3. Everyone is free to share thoughts and feelings. However we will not talk over one another or engage in conversations in the group that exclude others. We will not attempt to fix each other (only God can do that), and we will respectfully allow time for others to share.

Small Group Format

1. Begin your time with prayer to quiet the group and acknowledge God as your source of help and comfort.
2. Guide members through each week's discussion topics from the workbook.
3. Encourage members to share experiences and observations with the group. Take notes and write freely in this study guide.
4. End each session with prayer, lifting the group's petitions to God as a sign of hope.

Author's Close

There are more than 40 million caregivers in the United States alone. Most of us are overwhelmed, exhausted, and isolated. Some caregivers even experience stress levels on par with post-traumatic stress disorder. Caring for someone with exceptional needs affects finances, relationships, faith, as well as emotional and personal health.

As a leader of a caregiver small group, you are indeed a missionary, taking God's Word into an overlooked and forgotten land. People are concerned with the ones who are sick, but those who are doing the day-to-day caring are often forgotten. Please know that I am praying for you and your group members, that God will use you mightily to help the world remember the high honor of the calling to love and serve—the very calling of Jesus.

Chapter 1
EXPLORING PEACE

I have told you these things, so that in me you may have peace.
In this world you will have trouble. But take heart!
I have overcome the world.

—JOHN 16:33

What steals your peace? I think most of us can describe what steals our peace better than we can describe what peace is. There's a lot that keeps you irritated, worried, even angry—bad drivers, lazy kids, politics, potholes, your neighbors, physical pain, finances, telemarketers, in-laws, spiders, and on and on.

So let's start there. Write it all down: people, situations, things, etc. that steal your peace. It's important to take time to consider fully. Use extra paper if you need to. You don't have to share this with anyone you don't want to, but you will start feeling tension release by just getting this all out in the light.

Now let's take it to the next level. What are some of your emotions—grief, envy, shame, fear, guilt, loneliness, rejection, unforgiveness, and especially relevant in this age of social media—FOMO (fear of missing out)—that might be keeping you from experiencing peace? Write out your peace-stealing emotions.

As caregivers we have circumstances, responsibilities, and emotions that are especially overwhelming. What might those be for you (i.e., family members who won't help, Medicaid paperwork, IEP meetings, etc.)?

With all of this irritation and upset in our lives, peace seems like an enigma. How can anyone truly have peace when we seem powerless to change the things and people that bother us? There are some things that bother us simply *because* we cannot change them!

Peace is not just an ideal that's presented in the Bible; it's a way of living that God promises.

> *The LORD gives strength to his people; the LORD blesses*
> *his people with peace.*
>
> —PSALM 29:11

> *The fruit of that righteousness will be peace; its effect will be quietness*
> *and confidence forever. My people will live in peaceful dwelling*
> *places, in secure homes, in undisturbed places of rest.*
>
> —ISAIAH 32:17–18

> *Peace I leave with you; my peace I give you. I do not give to*
> *you as the world gives. Do not let your hearts be troubled*
> *and do not be afraid.*
>
> —JOHN 14:27

> *And the peace of God, which transcends all understanding, will guard*
> *your hearts and your minds in Christ Jesus.*
>
> —PHILIPPIANS 4:7

In this study we'll come to understand:

- Peace is possible, regardless of our circumstances because:
- God is the source of peace, and He freely gives it.
- But it's up to us to choose peace.

Peace is often seen as freedom from disturbance, as quiet and tranquility. However the most profound and comprehensive description of peace, or *shalom*, is what we'll explore in this book—a cosmic order ordained by God. In this cosmic order each part finds its meaning and function as it conforms to God's purpose. Things may not be easy, but you can always have peace.

Over generations, humans have come to believe we're independent creatures— separate from God (needing to behave and barter with Him), in competition with others, having forgotten our true identity and purpose. Until we remember who we are, whose we are, and why we're here, peace will elude us.

That's what we'll work on in this study, the inner healing or self-care that can change everything—learning (or remembering) you true identity and the resources that are available to you. Only when we know that truth can we experience success, fulfillment, wholeness, completeness, security, well-being, and harmony (i.e., peace).

As a caregiver, when we talk about peace, what is it we're really looking for? The suffering to stop for our loved one? An end to the sadness or depression? Someone else to take over the endless lists of responsibilities? A better relationship with the person we're caring for? What would peace look like for you?

If you can't change the course of the disease or disability, if you can't change other people, if you can't change your finances, if you have to do this by yourself, can you still have peace?

We're going to work on how you can have peace regardless of circumstances, because most things (situations, people) that steal your peace will probably not change, at least not to your complete satisfaction. If you haven't done the inner-healing work, the self-care, you'll always be plagued by dissatisfaction, resentment, frustration, and bitterness.

Loving and caring for a child, a spouse, a parent, or a friend should be a good thing, right? A rich and rewarding experience. Yet there's statistical proof that caregivers tend to neglect their own spiritual, emotional, and physical health,[1] suffer stress levels equal with post-traumatic stress disorder (PTSD), experience depression,[2] and have increased mortality risk.[3] Men, women, and even children are affected. And the numbers of caregivers are on the rise as 77 million Baby Boomers turn sixty-five and older, and disabilities now affect one in seven children.

Why is caring for others such a huge drain on our health and well-being? Some resources site lack of sleep, increased stress, loneliness, long-term exposure to suffering, lack of exercise and improper nutrition as causes. But what if we don't have the time or the resources to change our circumstances? What are some strategies you're currently adopting to improve your well-being (mental and physical)?

There are numerous resources for caregivers that offer methods to avoid caregiver burnout, compassion fatigue, depression, etc., but not everything that offers peace provides profound peace that can last through anything.

> *They dress the wound of my people as though it were not serious.*
> *"Peace, peace," they say, when there is no peace.*
>
> —*JEREMIAH 6:14*

> *Because they lead my people astray, saying, "Peace," when there is no*
> *peace, and because, when a flimsy wall is built, they cover it with*
> *whitewash, therefore tell those who cover it with whitewash that it*
> *is going to fall.*
>
> —*EZEKIEL 13:10–11*

Some popular and reasonable suggestions for getting a grip on the stresses of caregiving include

- making your health a priority with proper nutrition and exercise;
- practicing gratitude and forgiveness;

- learning to ask for and receive help from others; and
- joining a support group.

These are important things for a caregiver to do, but they're only "whitewash on a flimsy wall." If we want to enjoy loving and caring for others, do it with peace and patience, and not have it destroy our health, we must gain the proper perspective.

In order to do that we must be willing to change. *Yes, it's you that must change before anything will get better.* That's a hard concept to grasp because it seems as though there are many other people and situations that need to change before you can have peace. Such as:

- The disease or disability needs to go away.
- The person we're caring for needs to shape up. Perhaps they have behavior issues or are just rude and ungrateful.
- Money needs to no longer be a problem. There's just not enough to hire quality care services or get the therapies needed.
- Relatives need to stop being judgmental and start jumping in to help.
- The "system" (i.e. school, hospital, government) needs to stop failing you.
- God needs to start answering your prayers.

Take a moment to look back on your own list of who or what is stealing your peace. Now brace yourself for the shocking truth. *No one and nothing can steal your peace unless you give it the power to!* The only one who can affect your peace is you.

In the coming chapters we're going to learn how to choose peace. It's going to require that you change your perspective. That can be very hard to do, but consider the pain and heartache of your current perspective. Don't you want to be free of frustration, anger, and guilt?

Here are some challenges you may face when changing your perspective:

Addiction to Victimization: This world teaches us to blame others for our problems and not take personal responsibility. It's hard to no longer blame the disease or disability, the difficult attitude of the person you care for, the failures of "the system," etc. and instead take responsibility for your own peace.

Pride: Great humility is required to have inner peace. There will be times in this process where you'll need to swallow your pride and give up your need to be right or to "win" in order to remain in relationship with someone.

Control: God is in control of everyone and everything, not you. Allowing things or people to be as they are will seem unreasonable, even ridiculous, but it's the only way to let Him work it out for what's right for all involved.

Status Quo: Painful as things can be now, they're familiar and somewhat safe. Letting go of old habits and patterns can be terrifying when shifting from our way to His way.

Identity with Pain: All else may be shifting and changing, but one thing seems constant—pain. If you've allowed any part of yourself to become invested in your emotional and spiritual pain, you will resist every attempt to heal that pain. It's become a part of you.

Compassion means "to suffer with," but for some of us, being compassionate has driven us to "suffering *more than*." Your loved one may be a precious, innocent child, a loving spouse, or a kind and quiet elder, but in caring for them you've become an overwhelmed, exhausted, impatient hot mess. What's happening?

Before we can join others in their suffering, we need to have recognized and made peace with our own brokenness, otherwise their pain will trigger our hot spots, and you'll find yourself losing control over the seemingly smallest things. Have you ever flipped out over how someone chews their food? Have you ever shouted angrily, "Hurry up!" to your loved one who can only shuffle? Have you ever refused to take your loved one to the bathroom "because *no one* could possibly need to go three times in an hour"?

Being a peaceful caregiver is possible, but we must learn more about who we are, why we're here, and the power we have available to us to do the good work we were created to do.

Prayer

Lord, there is much on my plate, and I feel overwhelmed, not only by my responsibilities but by my emotions. I come to You, Lord, for peace and comfort—not as the world gives but only as You can.

Chapter 2
FINDING OUR TRUE ID

For we are God's handiwork, created in Christ Jesus to do good works, which God prepared in advance for us to do.

—*EPHESIANS 2:10*

Humanity has searched high and low for the meaning of life, our reason for being, yet it's clear—we're created by God for His purposes and pleasure. He created us in His image (Genesis 1:27), meaning we find our inherent identity in Him. Just as He created seed to bring forth its kind (i.e., apple seed brings forth an apple, marigold seed brings forth a marigold, vv. 11–12), God created us in His image to bring forth or be an expression of Him on this earth. He even invited us to take His name (Colossians 3:17) and function in His power (Isaiah 40:29; Ephesians 3:20).

Yet fallen humankind, believing ourselves to be separated from God, searches for other means of acceptance and worth, forgetting the value that comes with just being His.

We've come to believe we exist to accumulate wealth and possessions, perhaps receive some notoriety, have enjoyable experiences, and love family and friends. But Jesus came to show us we're created for so much more!

Very truly I tell you, whoever believes in me will do the works I have been doing, and they will do even greater things than these, because I am going to the Father.

—*JOHN 14:12*

Do you see yourself that way? Do you believe you were created to good works that God prepared in advance for you to do? Even greater things than Jesus did? What you believe about yourself defines the experience you have in this life.

As he thinks within himself, so he is.

—PROVERBS 23:7 NASB

Are you a child of God, loved, protected, and provided for? Or are you on your own, having to do the hard work, responsible for everything and everyone? It's difficult to choose peace when you perceive your situation that way.

You may not be able to change your circumstances, but what if you could say to yourself at all times: *No matter how hard this seems, I've been created by God for such a time as this. He has not abandoned me. He is here with me to help me realize who I truly am, not who I thought I was, and to help me see others as they truly are, not as I judge them to be. I choose to be at peace and trust Him to lead me, lead us, to green pastures and still waters.*

That kind of thinking takes a shift in perspective about who you are and why you're here. In this chapter we're going to create a life-changing visual that will help you understand how you can make the shift and function from a new perspective, a place of peace.

Body

When we're born, there are some very specific things about us that, for the most part, we can't change. Take some time to consider the physical traits and aspects (not opinions, but facts) that make you *you*, and write them inside the human figure on page 13.

SPIRIT

FLESH

EGO

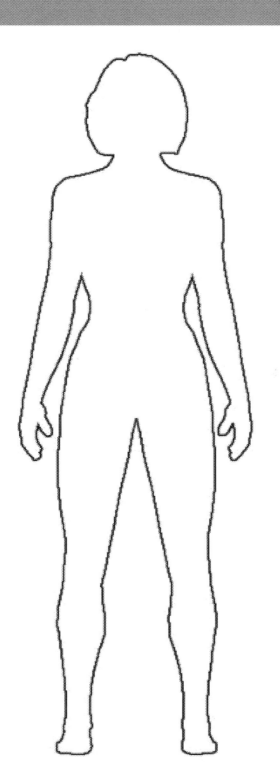

Here are some ideas to get you started:

- Your genealogy or your family tree/relatives
- The generation you are born into
- Your nationality or race
- Your genetic make-up
- Your blood type

We are living, breathing vessels with unique features, known by God who placed us on this earth during a specific time, in a certain place, for Him to use for a special purpose.

> *For you created my inmost being; you knit me together*
> *in my mother's womb.*
>
> *—PSALM 139:13*

> *And even the very hairs of your head are all numbered.*
>
> *—MATTHEW 10:30*

> *From one man he made all the nations, that they should inhabit the*
> *whole earth; and he marked out their appointed times in history*
> *and the boundaries of their lands.*
>
> *—ACTS 17:26*

God created our bodies as vessels for Him to inhabit (1 Corinthians 3:16) and gave us minds in order to learn, make choices and decisions, and interpret our world as safe or dangerous, to run or stay, to go straight or turn left.

In His wisdom, God also instituted a labeling system of all He created so we would be able to interpret and navigate His creation. Man, woman, plant, animal, land, and sea. He called it all good. He even brought the living creatures to the man for him to name them (Genesis 2:19). We are still labeling things to this day so that our minds can process, categorize, and interpret.

To the right of the human figure, under FLESH, list some of the factual (not subjective) labels you might use when describing yourself.

1. Where you live—i.e., the South, Europe, South Bronx, uptown, downtown, etc.
2. Marital status—married, widowed, divorced, etc.
3. Religion—Christian, Jewish, Southern Baptist, Buddhist, etc.
4. Political preference—Republican, moderate, Democrat, etc.
5. Financial status—middle class, wealthy, retired, etc.
6. Body type—tall, skinny, round, muscular, etc.
7. Profession—artist, teacher, lawyer, acupuncturist, etc.

These might be the facts that label each one of us, but how those labels are interpreted by ourselves and others is where the trouble begins.

Flesh/Ego

We're all taught things from a variety of sources—parents, religion, experiences, culture, etc.—that mold and shape our thoughts, opinions, and actions. As a result we can all be in the same physical world but have very different interpretations of what we behold. What is beautiful to one can be ugly to another. What appears safe to one can appear to be dangerous to another.

Imagine you're going to meet someone you've never met before at a coffee shop. The person has been described as a tall, white, Southern, divorced, Catholic, Democrat, middle class, male teacher. You can see him in your mind's eye, and without even meeting him, you start forming opinions based on your experiences or what you've been taught to think about such a person. "He sounds charming," or "Yuck!" It's the algorithm for matchmaking online. But we're doing it all day long—sizing people up, forming opinions, even judging them based on labels.

On dating apps, the algorithm is meant to lead us to the perfect match, promising harmony, even love. But in reality, most of our opinions and judgments create division, even conflict and war. We use our labels to prove we are different, separate, in competition, not in community. How did this happen? How did what God labeled as good become a battleground?

In Genesis we read the story of the fall of man. In the Garden of Eden was the tree of life and the tree of the knowledge of good and evil (Genesis 2:9). Even though Adam and Eve had been warned of the danger of eating from the tree of knowledge, the desire to know and make decisions for themselves easily overruled their desire to be obedient to God. They wanted the power of knowing for themselves instead of just trusting God. So they ate. And in an instant they went from walking naked with God, feeling no shame, to hiding from God, feeling separated and guilty.

The mind is a gift. Free will is a gift. But when we decide that we must know so *we* can have the final say, we've chosen pride, power, ego, and flesh (what is seen) over God, love, trust, and faith (what is unseen, Hebrews 11:1). We've chosen to let the ego or flesh direct our mind instead of the Spirit of our Creator. The result is our world today.

The mind governed by the flesh is death, but the mind governed
by the Spirit is life and peace.

—*ROMANS 8:6*

With our egos running the show, we have developed a false perception of ourselves and others. Our ego tells us we are independent creatures—separate from God and in competition with others—for power, for provision, for love and acceptance. We fall from abundance, community, and love into fear, isolation, and lack. The good news is—there's a way home.

In a garden, Adam chose his own will over God's. In a garden, Jesus prayed, "Yet not as I will, but as you will" (Matthew 26:39), showing us the Way.

Still writing to the right side of the body chart, start another list under EGO. List some of the ways the ego interprets labels. These subjective labels can also be called judgments.

1. Accepted or rejected
2. Dumb or smart
3. Able or disabled
4. Conqueror or victim
5. Ugly or beautiful
6. Worthy or unworthy
7. Success or failure
8. Accepted or condemned
9. Mean or nice
10. Lovable or unlovable

What are some of the labels/judgments you've put on yourself?

What are some of the judgments you've put on the person(s) you're caring for?

What are some of the judgments you've put on your peace stealers (i.e., the therapist is mean, my sister-in-law is a wimp, the doctor is an idiot)?

Whether or not these labels are true (let's hope your doctor is not an idiot!), they influence our attitudes and emotions. These thoughts/judgments from ego's labels of people and circumstances are unfortunately more often negative than positive. We tend to size up the "threat" of something or someone more readily than we do the benefit. We focus on and remember the negative in order to be able to recognize and protect ourselves from the things that can harm us. So these negative thoughts about ourselves and others become the chatter in our minds that run our lives!

Negative thought chatter is referred to as the work of the father of lies. If you are always looking for what's wrong and judging people and situations from a negative perspective, you are creating a world of low self-esteem, suspicion, and fear with the stress of always having to be on your guard for predators and idiots. That's no way to live!

You belong to your father, the devil, and you want to carry out your father's desires. He was a murderer from the beginning, not holding to the truth, for there is no truth in him. When he lies, he speaks his native language, for he is a liar and the father of lies.

—JOHN 8:44

The thief comes only to steal and kill and destroy; I [Jesus] have come that they may have life, and have it to the full.

—JOHN 10:10

We've learned that there are many influencers that help mold and shape who we are and how we think—family, culture, labels, ego, and mindset— some factual and some purely subjective, but all with powerful influence. Consider the difference it makes when a person describes themselves as overlooked, rejected, unworthy, and unimportant versus loved, welcomed, worthy, and valuable. With labels come beliefs, and with beliefs come emotions, opinions, and actions.

When it becomes difficult to be you, you might pursue psychology, therapy, counsel, and even medication to ease the pain, quiet the chaos, and make sense of it all. When we have lost our way, become overwhelmed, or succumbed to depression, getting help is imperative.

But the help will only have a temporary effect if the ego is still in control. If we want peace, lasting peace, it's important that we have the correct operating system guiding our thoughts, helping us process and interpret what's going on. Most of us have given our egos full access to govern our decisions and thoughts. But God's Word tells us there's another source for guidance.

Spirit

> *But it is the spirit in a person, the breath of the Almighty,*
> *that gives them understanding.*
>
> —*Job 32:8*

> *But the Advocate, the Holy Spirit, whom the Father will send in my*
> *name, will teach you all things and will remind you of everything I*
> *have said to you.*
>
> —*John 14:26*

> *But when he, the Spirit of truth, comes, he will guide you into*
> *all the truth.*
>
> —*John 16:13*

God breathed life into us (Genesis 2:7) and has freely given us His Spirit through grace, but it's up to us to choose which will run our lives—Spirit or flesh (read Romans 8:1–17 and Galatians 5:16–26). In the flesh we see ourselves as separated from God, in competition with and fearful of others. However, regardless of our race, education, nationality, ability, socio-economic classification, etc., God sees us as His beloved children, not condemned but saved, loved, and forgiven, having purpose and value.

We believe it is through the grace of our Lord Jesus that we are saved.

—ACTS *15:11*

For it is by grace you have been saved, through faith—and this is not from yourselves, it is the gift of God—not by works, so that no one can boast.

—EPHESIANS *2:8–9*

Spend some time with the following Scripture passages, and then, to the left of the body diagram, under SPIRIT, write these and all other terms you find to describe you as God describes those who believe Him. Also, read Ephesians 1:3–14 for more good news about who you are.

Genesis 1:26—Made in His Image
1 Samuel 12:22; 1 Corinthians 6:19—His Own
Jeremiah 1:5—Known
Matthew 5:14—Light of the World
John 1:12—Child of God
John 15:15—Friend
Romans 15:7—Accepted

2 Corinthians 5:17—New Creation
2 Corinthians 6:16—Temple of the Living God
Galatians 5:1—Free
Ephesians 1:4—Chosen
Colossians 2:10—Complete
1 Thessalonians 1:4—Loved
2 Peter 1:4—Divine

If you believe what God says is true about you, and if you allowed His Holy Spirit to guide you, how differently might you feel about yourself and others? How would that affect your life?

Review the body diagram. You can see that we all tend to view ourselves and others from the ego's point view, identifying with those familiar labels. But what this life-changing visual clearly reveals is the difference between the reality of who God says we are and who we *think* we are. Above EGO, label the right side "False Self." Above SPIRIT, label the left side "True Self."

So if we were created to be one way, but we're living our lives in opposition to that, no wonder it's hard for us to find peace and purpose! No wonder we feel confused and stressed. We've disconnected from our very reason for being. We've been listening to the wrong voice and trusting in the wrong source.

This visual can help us more clearly see there are two forces influencing our lives—but one of them is eternally true (Spirit) and the other is fickle and false (ego). To some degree you've been aware of this dichotomy your whole life. Maybe it's not an angel on one shoulder and a devil on the other, but we've all been made aware of the conflict within.

Perhaps you've experienced that conflict when you know what you should do, but you don't want to do it. Or perhaps you've been trying to concentrate, and disruptive thoughts keep popping up. If you're trying to concentrate, where are the disruptive thoughts coming from? We've all said, "So I asked myself . . ." Who is the *I* that is asking the *self*?

As caregivers we're placed in very difficult circumstances that weaken our resolve to cling to what we know is True: watching someone suffer, making personal sacrifices to serve others, making life and death decisions for another, spending hours alone at a bedside. In these situations, our egos can run amok, telling us this is unfair, no one else cares, this a waste of valuable time, and God has turned His back on us. These are all lies and leave us feeling broken and overwhelmed.

Peace comes from discovering your true identity as the child of a loving God, quieting the voice of your ego, and allowing the Holy Spirit to guide you in Truth. What does God think about you, your situation, and the person you care for? In the next chapter we'll discover the benefits of a life run by the Holy Spirit instead of ego.

Prayer

Lord, I'm confused. I've believed lies about myself and others for a long time. Who am I and why am I here? What does caregiving have to do with it? Give me eyes to see, ears to hear, and a heart to understand from Your perspective that I may have peace.

Chapter 3
LIFE IN THE SPIRIT

So I say, walk by the Spirit, and you will not gratify the desires of the flesh. For the flesh desires what is contrary to the Spirit, and the Spirit what is contrary to the flesh.

—*GALATIANS 5:16–17*

In chapter one we explored the fact that you're going to need to shift your perspective in order to have peace in all circumstances. In chapter two we developed a visual to help you shift perspective and be aware that you have a choice between Spirit or ego. In this chapter we're going to explore the benefits of life in the Spirit, how the Spirit brings us back in line with our original design and therefore back to *shalom*, or the peace and satisfaction of being in sync with God's plan for your life.

Remember Why You're Here

God created you in His image for His purposes. There is good work God prepared in advance for you to do. Just like Jesus had an assignment, so do you and so does the person you care for. You will probably never fully understand your purpose and value on the earth right now, but one day you will (1 Corinthians 13:12). No matter what you thought you were here to do, it's God's will for your life that prevails (Proverbs 19:21).

Do you not know that your bodies are temples of the Holy Spirit, who is in you, whom you have received from God? You are not your own; you were bought at a price.

—*1 Corinthians 6:19–20*

In him we were also chosen, having been predestined according to the plan of him who works out everything in conformity with the purpose of his will.

—*Ephesians 1:11*

For it is God who works in you to will and to act in order to fulfill his good purpose.

—*Philippians 2:13*

Do you believe that where you are, what you're doing, and the trials you're facing are not a mistake? Take a moment to identify any areas where you see evidence of His hand at work in your circumstances.

If this is true for you, can you see that it must be true for the person you're caring for as well? It may be difficult to look at a suffering loved one and believe God's perfect and loving will is being done, but then we must turn our eyes to

Jesus on the Cross. He didn't end up there by mistake. There was God-ordained purpose in every aspect of Jesus' life—even the suffering. God's ways are not our ways (Isaiah 55:8–9). What appears to be rejection, failure, or defeat can be used for greatness in God's hands.

Just because we pray, we're obedient, and we're His, doesn't mean we don't suffer. But when we have life in the Spirit, His will and purpose become more important than the suffering (Matthew 26:36–42; 2 Corinthians 11:16–33).

He went away a second time and prayed, "My Father, if it is
not possible for this cup to be taken away unless I drink it, may your
will be done."

—*MATTHEW 26:42*

We are all His, but according to the world's terms, people who are intellectually challenged, old and frail, or lying in a coma, are described as having no life. They appear to have lost their value, yet in God's kingdom, it's those who lose their life who find it (Matthew 16:25). Christ's power anoints those who are weak (2 Corinthians 12:9). He uses the weak to shame the strong and the foolish to shame the wise (1 Corinthians 1:27).

What if God is healing you, drawing you nearer to Him through your loved one? What if people watching your patient and loving care are being touched by God in their hearts? What if as you love and serve you reveal the purpose and value of those the world dehumanizes?

Dear children, let us not love with words or speech but with
actions and in truth.

—*1 JOHN 3:18*

In God's economy every moment of every life has purpose and meaning and value. Learning to love and care through this lens gives great importance to this good work God prepared in advance for you to do.

Changing Your Operating System

The man-made, ego-driven infrastructure of this world is failing us. The systems and institutions of education, capitalism, government, medicine, etc. are collapsing as we have forgotten that our most important purpose is expressing our God-given divinity and dominion by loving and caring for others and the planet.

We're here by God's will for His purposes. We know His Spirit is working in us and available to guide us. But we've been listening to our ego and the world for too long. It's become familiar and easy. We've formed opinions and created relationships based on lies. We don't like the results, but we've become addicted to the patterns of judging, being offended, worrying, being resentful, etc. Ego tempts you constantly to resort to old patterns and habits, but you're not trapped (James 4:1). You're not a victim. You don't have to succumb to those thoughts. You may be tempted, but there is a way out. Jesus knows what it's like to hear the voice of the ego that tells you lies and steals your peace. His life exemplifies one that's obedient to Spirit, not to ego—despite temptation.

> *Do not conform to the pattern of this world, but be transformed by the renewing of your mind. Then you will be able to test and approve what God's will is—his good, pleasing and perfect will.*
>
> *—ROMANS 12:2*

> *No temptation [testing] has overtaken you except what is common to mankind. And God is faithful; he will not let you be tempted beyond what you can bear. But when you are tempted, he will also provide* a way out *so that you can endure it.*
>
> *—1 CORINTHIANS 10:13 (EMPHASIS ADDED)*

*You were taught, with regard to your former way of life, to put off
your old self, which is being corrupted by its deceitful desires; to be
made new in the attitude of your minds; and to put on the new self,
created to be like God in true righteousness and holiness.*

—*EPHESIANS 4:22–24*

*Because he himself suffered when he was tempted, he is able to help
those who are being tempted.*

—*HEBREWS 2:18*

Shifting from ego to Spirit, renewing your mind, and dying to self can be a
difficult if not terrifying process. Have you ever tried to go from working on a
PC or Microsoft computer operating system to using a Mac or Apple operating
system? Until you get the hang of the new system you can get quite frustrated
and lost. It's the same when you go from letting your ego run your mind to
allowing the Spirit to take over.

The driving force that schedules your daily routines, sets the tone for your
relationships, manages your finances, inspires your health practices, and sets your
expectations for the future changes, and suddenly your firm foundation becomes
shifting sands. Things that used to be important no longer are. Relationships
and routines get reprioritized and reorganized.

With ego in charge:
- Daily routine may have been a tight schedule of work and housekeeping
  with little down time for family or fitness.
- Relationships may have been strained and difficult with much effort
  exerted to prove yourself right.
- Finances may have focused on the ability to acquire more and prepare for
  retirement.

- Fast and processed food kept you and your family on your tight schedule.
- Expectations were high—demanding peak performance and perfection from everyone.

With Spirit in charge:
- Your job is now the care of another. "Neat and tidy" will do.
- You have let go of your need to be right in order to be in relationship.
- There is room in the budget to help others.
- Nutrition is important to the health and healing of both you and your loved one.
- You're grateful and content with what you have.

What old habits, patterns, even plans have you had to let go of or change in order to be a caregiver?

❈

Changing over to a Spirit-led life can also be difficult because we live in a world built by human intellect and reasoning. It functions from a material perspective (flesh), and we are being called to function from Spirit. Those still operating by the patterns of this world just can't understand.

Scenario: Instead of being a "helicopter" caregiver, you've stopped hovering so much and learned to trust more. You've allowed your husband with dementia a little more freedom (let him choose his own clothes even if they don't match, let him miss a therapy session to enjoy an outing, etc.), but your sister-in-law now thinks *you* have dementia!

Scenario: Perhaps you've forgiven an old friend and extended grace instead of being bitter and resentful. In the renewed spirit of friendship, your friend picks your kids up from soccer while you're at a doctor's appointment with your mother. Your husband is confused and wants to know what new drugs *you* are on!

Scenario: Your child with severe intellectual and physical challenges needs a difficult surgery. Although there's pressure to act quickly, you tell the doctor that you need some time to pray with your child and the entire family in order to know God's will. Acknowledging that God is in charge—not you, the doctor, or your mother—has brought a new level of peace for everyone.

This new system gives us permission to slow down, rest, and hear from God. Ego has us constantly on the go, striving, working, pushing, to get more, prove our worthiness, impress people. Yet, "This is what the Sovereign LORD, the Holy One of Israel, says: 'In repentance and rest is your salvation, in quietness and trust is your strength, but you would have none of it'" (Isaiah 30:15).

In this Scripture Isaiah used the word *repentance.* In the New Testament Jesus calls us to repent many times. The word He uses is derived from the Greek *metanoeó*, which means to change one's mind. Perhaps He is saying, "Change the operating system of your mind from ego to Spirit." Jesus came to change our operating system so we could have rest, quietness, and peace all by just trusting Him. What a switch!

What specific ways could this new operating system help you make peace with caregiving?

Rely on His Spirit in You

Changing operating systems takes faith. Do you remember the scene from the movie *Indiana Jones and the Last Crusade* where Indy must cross a great chasm, yet there is no apparent means to cross? He refers to the sacred text he's carrying and realizes the next step must be a leap of faith. As he takes the first terrifying step, he can then see that there is, indeed, a narrow but sturdy bridge across the chasm.

In much the same way we must take that step of faith, trusting the Holy Spirit. We must learn to no longer rely on worldly reasoning but rather trust in what is unseen over what appears to be real. That sounds hard to do, but in reality, you trust unseen divine intelligence every day. Without your striving or willing it to happen—your heart beats, your lungs breath, your gut digests, your skin heals up. Without your striving, the sun comes up, the seasons change, fruit grows, and trees make oxygen and consume harmful carbon dioxide. Amazing!

Trust in the LORD with all your heart and lean not on
your own understanding.

—PROVERBS 3:5

*The person without the Spirit does not accept the things that
come from the Spirit of God but considers them foolishness,
and cannot understand them because they are discerned only
through the Spirit.*

—*1 Corinthians 2:14*

For those who are willing to ask and receive, the Holy Spirit actually dwells in us to guide and direct our lives (Acts 2:38).

*I in them and you in me—so that they may be brought to
complete unity.*

—*John 17:23*

*I have been crucified with Christ and I no longer live, but Christ
lives in me.*

—*Galatians 2:20*

*Because the one who is in you is greater than the one who
is in the world.*

—*1 John 4:4*

When we change operating systems we realize we don't have to "conjure" the Holy Spirit. He's *always* present to not only guide but also to provide wisdom—even to discern the will of God!

*We continually ask God to fill you with the knowledge of his will
through all the wisdom and understanding that the Spirit gives.*

—*Colossians 1:9*

When caring for another we're often required to make decisions that seem difficult if not downright impossible—putting someone in a home, allowing surgery, changing meds, taking someone off life support, etc. You can try and figure it out by reasoning and intellect, but when you come to a decision and things don't turn out as you planned, you carry the guilt.

However, when you've learned to rely on the ever-present Holy Spirit, all you need do is pray, "Thy will be done." You can have confidence that His perfect will, will be done and have no guilt, even if things don't turn out the way you expected or wanted. The comfort and peace will come when you're willing to let go of your expectations, believe that God is in control, accept what is happening, and trust in God's goodness to get you through it.

List the decisions that require your attention right now. After each one write, "Thy will be done."

There are many times when we're so weak and weary that we don't even know what to pray. His Spirit intercedes for us. Rest in the peace of that! We don't even have to know how to pray or have the energy to pray when we have surrendered to His Holy Spirit.

In the same way, the Spirit helps us in our weakness. We do not know what we ought to pray for, but the Spirit himself intercedes for us through wordless groans. And he who searches our hearts knows the mind of the Spirit, because the Spirit intercedes for God's people in accordance with the will of God.

—*ROMANS 8:26–27*

What peace! His Spirit is present, available, and powerful. All we need to pray is, "Thy will be done."

Prayer

Lord, I'm beginning to see that there is another way to perceive, another way to live. Making the change from old thoughts and patterns will be difficult, even scary. Hold me close. Let me see Your Spirit at work that I may learn to rest and trust more and more.

Chapter 4

PRACTICING PEACE: PART ONE

Whatever you have learned or received or heard from me, or seen in me—put it into practice. And the God of peace will be with you.

—*PHILIPPIANS 4:9*

It's evident now that peace is possible for us when we learn to choose Spirit over flesh/ego. But we've been operating from ego for a long time. Putting newly discovered insights into practice within the realm of day-to-day living will help us to close the gap between knowing peace is possible and realizing peace. In these next two chapters (divided so you can spend more time on each section), we'll explore five ways you can "practice" peace—awareness, stillness, emptying, listening, and praying.

Awareness

Just in the last few chapters you've been made aware of things that may have been hidden from you in the past:

- Things that are stealing your peace.
- You've been judging yourself and others based on ego/man-made labels.
- You have a choice between Spirit and ego.
- Peace is a choice.

What are some other concepts or principles of which this study has made you aware? Concepts like these can fade over time. Take time to write them down so you can revisit and remember until they become reality to you.

One of the most powerful benefits of developing awareness is realizing that you can control your thoughts and change them. You can choose to see things a different way. You can quiet the old mental chatter of negativity and shame and change it to joy and self-acceptance. What's happening to you may not change, but how you think about what's happening can. Like Paul we can learn to "count it all joy."

> *My brethren, count it all joy when you fall into various trials.*
>
> ### —JAMES 1:2 NKJV

Becoming aware that there's more to you than the endless stream of thoughts parading through your mind is a subtle but game-changing insight. By stepping out of your thoughts and into awareness, by becoming a studious observer of your thoughts, you'll have the means to find peace.

Maybe someone says something hurtful to you. Your old self lets that trigger the ego to take over. Memories, shame, labels, etc. cause you pain. You're indignant, offended, and wounded. You react from that pain. Perhaps you storm from the room. Maybe you say hurtful things back or just break down in tears.

When the ego's in charge, you'll probably just make matters worse. Your response will cause more pain and build the wall of separation even higher.

However the more aware you become of your thoughts, the more you can take them "captive to the mind of Christ." Go back to our body diagram in the last chapter. On the True Self side, write "mind of Christ."

> *For, "Who has known the mind of the Lord so as to instruct him?"*
> *But we have the mind of Christ.*
>
> *—1 CORINTHIANS 2:16*

> *We demolish arguments and every pretension that sets itself up*
> *against the knowledge of God, and we take captive every thought to*
> *make it obedient to Christ.*
>
> *—2 CORINTHIANS 10:5*

Like Jesus we can choose a more wise and righteous response when we're aware that we can pause and let the Spirit tell us what to do. Yes, this takes practice! The next time someone hurts you, you may realize for a split second, "Okay, I don't have to shout back," or, "Don't cry," but you do it anyway because that's what you've always done, and it feels familiar. But the next time you come to that crossroads you'll realize you have a choice and hesitate just a bit longer. Eventually you'll come to that crossroads and learn to wait and let a new thought emerge that offers a new response. Hence the age-old wisdom of taking a deep breath and counting to ten.

Awareness that you have a choice and the willingness to hear the Spirit will trigger a new response that can change the trajectory of relationships and the level of peace in your life.

Think of a time when you blurted out something hurtful to the person you care for. Consider the consequences. Now imagine what you might have said or how different things may have been if you had chosen your words more carefully or didn't say anything at all.

Stillness

By observing and not immediately reacting, you're gaining control over your thoughts. Just a split-second pause or stillness creates space where new thoughts and new reactions spring up. It's in the stillness between thought and reaction that you allow the influence of Spirit over ego.

The Lord will fight for you; you need only to be still.

—EXODUS 14:14

He says, "Be still, and know that I am God."

—PSALM 46:10

See, I am doing a new thing! Now it springs up; do you not perceive it? I am making a way in the wilderness and streams in the wasteland.

—ISAIAH 43:19

It's in quieting the chatter of the ego that we can hear the voice of God; however getting your mind to a place of stillness is easier said than done.

Try this. Sit down in a quiet place with the intention of stillness and peace for just two minutes. Set the timer on your phone. Close your eyes and don't move from the chair until the alarm sounds. Now remember, your intention is stillness and peace. You'll almost immediately become aware of how hard it is to sit in the quiet. The chatter of the ego will chime in.

What am I doing? I have so much to do. Well, it's only two minutes. I can spare that much time. Mmmmm. I smell coffee. I should have brought a cup in here with me. Wait! Is that coffee or is something burning? Oh, good Lord! It smells like burning socks! No, but I didn't turn the dryer on. But I did put the clothes in the dryer last night. Yuck. They're probably mildewing. I need to remember to check, but I'll forget. I need to write that down, but I didn't bring a notepad. This is ridiculous! I have too much to do to be sitting here like an idiot. Time's got to be nearly up.

Only thirty-two seconds have gone by, and you're already irritated, and yet another to-do list is forming!

Why can't we quiet the ego? Quite frankly it's because the ego is an enemy of stillness. Let's explore a few reasons why.

Competition: Experts tell us the amount of information that's thrown at us each day is way too much for us to realistically process (advertising, emails, news, Facebook, let alone work, school, etc.). Yet we feel like we have to know or else we'll miss out or be left behind. Turning it all off or unplugging, even for a short amount of time, seems unrealistic.

Safety: Because we believe we carry full responsibility (for ourselves and others), we're always on high alert. (Did she take her meds? Was that a seizure? What if the chemo doesn't work? He might fall. What if our money runs out?) If you're not "what-iffing" or worrying, you're afraid of what might happen. Spending time being still feels not only wrong but unsafe.

Guilt: Again, because we believe we carry full responsibility for everything and everyone, taking time for ourselves to be still brings guilt. The "should'ves and could'ves" take over. Instead of stillness being an important part of better care of yourself and others, it's a guilty and unnecessary indulgence.

Our situation is not hopeless, however. We can quiet the ego and gain control, but it takes practice. While it won't happen overnight, you will begin to almost immediately feel relief once you put it into practice.

Your first attempt at two minutes of quiet time may not have gone well, but don't let that stop you. Try the two minutes of stillness and peace again, but this time, use a notepad and pen. When the quiet begins, instead of listening to your thoughts and letting them lead you down a series of rabbit trails, jot a quick note about each thought then let it go and wait for the next thought. When the two minutes are over, go back and review. Your pad may read like this: *Birds. Quiet. Good pen. Hungry. What's in fridge? I hear my breath. Listening. Don't watch timer.*

To be able to write about the thought, the mind has to be able to process, categorize, edit, then write. These actions put the mind back in control and don't give the ego time to form opinions from old thoughts, habits, and patterns. When you come to know yourself as thought's witness, the mind is back in control and able to wait, listen, and then process and choose—what it was created to do!

Even if you have a hard time sitting still, you can quiet the ego while you're active, doing things you enjoy. Gardening, crossword puzzles, baking, dancing, etc. can be wonderful practices to help you become more mindful. They not only feed your joy and creativity, but you must focus on next steps, use your logic, and implement hand-eye coordination to get the job done. These are all essential skills your mind was created to do—not harbor bitterness, judge others, or throw a pity party!

Taking a little time each day to feed your joy and quiet the ego can be a life-changing practice in self-care. You will develop a stronger sense of self, purpose, and peace.

Chapter 5
PRACTICING PEACE: PART TWO

We're doing this study because we want to have peace. We're tired of being frustrated, impatient, and even angry at the person we're caring for. We don't want to feel sad or fearful any more. We're tired of resenting others and feeling sorry for ourselves. We want to change, but if change is to occur, we must let go of what's been holding us back. We must be willing to empty ourselves of past hurts, damaging feelings, and old stories to make room for the new thing God is willing to do in us.

> *Neither do people pour new wine into old wineskins. If they do, the skins will burst; the wine will run out and the wineskins will be ruined. No, they pour new wine into new wineskins, and both are preserved.*
>
> —*MATTHEW 9:17*

> *Who, being in very nature God, did not consider equality with God something to be used to his own advantage; rather, he made himself nothing by taking the very nature of a servant, being made in human likeness.*
>
> —*PHILIPPIANS 2:6–7*

Emptying

The Greek verb *kenoō* means to let go or to empty oneself, and this is the word Paul uses to describe the state Jesus chose when He "made himself nothing." Imagine Jesus willingly emptying Himself. The Son of God stepping down from glory and emptying Himself to take on the role of a servant.

What does Jesus willingly emptying Himself mean to you?

If we're constantly clinging to the past, trying to make old expectations fit the new situation, we'll never be content. Things just aren't going to be what you thought. Letting go of expectations and accepting the situation is the only way you'll be able to let Spirit guide you in peace.

No doubt you've needed to make major adjustments to your schedule—maybe even cancel a trip, quit a job, or move. Other than these kinds of changes, there are deep emotional and psychological changes taking place. Perhaps one of these situations is familiar.

Scenario: The man you thought would love and care for you can no longer remember your name and can no longer feed himself, let alone do all the chores he used to. He may no longer be what you expected a husband to be. He's a stranger, but he's still your husband.

Scenario: You were preparing your heart and home for a child who would be smart, obedient, energetic, and as cute and loveable as the other toddlers. Yet you find yourself with a child that still can't speak at age four and has strange, uncontrollable behaviors. Your child is struggling, rejected, and depressed—and so are you.

Scenario: You were the child. They were the parent. Now they're having a hard time letting you take care of them, making it awkward and downright difficult for everyone. They used to be in charge, and now you need to be.

After reading these scenarios, consider your situation. What are some expectations and old stories you might want to let go of to make room for the new thing God is doing?

Listening

> *Here's what I want: Give me a God-listening heart so I can lead your people well, discerning the difference between good and evil.*
>
> *—1 KINGS 3:9 THE MESSAGE*
>
> *Whether you turn to the right or to the left, your ears will hear a voice behind you, saying, "This is the way; walk in it."*
>
> *—ISAIAH 30:21*

Give ear and come to me; listen, that you may live.

—*Isaiah 55:3*

Imagine you're in a room full of people and everyone is talking. The speaker takes the stage to deliver a very important message, but no one quiets the room. No one hands him a microphone. He speaks anyway, and you seem to be the only one straining to hear him. You just can't seem to get what he's saying. It's like that for most of us when trying to hear the Spirit. We might want to hear from Him, but until we quiet the noise it's nearly impossible.

Not only is there noise from the constant chatter of your ego, but there's the noise of old expectations, the needs and opinions of others, social media, news, etc. That's why stillness and emptying must come first.

We're also straining to hear words that we can comprehend, process, and understand. Listening to the Spirit is not like that. He's not across the room talking at you, hoping you'll hear and understand well enough to go and do it.

- He speaks through revelation and inspiration—transcending words and understanding.
- He speaks through His Word.
- He speaks through His people—teachers, prophets, and witnesses.

His Holy Spirit dwells in you, and all you truly must do is say in trust and humility, "Yes, Lord. Thy will be done." Supernatural guidance will take over. It's not up to you. His Spirit is orchestrating everything—people, timing, providence, etc. to make it all work.

It's not only important to listen for the Spirit, but it's essential to listen to others if we are to love and care for them well.

Compassion is fueled by listening, by being able to hear and understand the needs and cries of others. Imagine the humiliation, confusion, even pain of being bathed, fed, dressed, and medicated by someone who's not listening to you.

Respect is fueled by listening. Listening to someone who is mentally ill, intellectually challenged, out of touch with reality, or with whom you disagree may seem like a waste of time or a threat to your position, but it is a gesture of respect—an open door connection and cooperation despite differences.

Reconciliation is fueled by listening. Even if we are two very different people, we can listen with compassion and respect to each other and find a way to reconciliation and relationship.

Recall a time when a parent, friend, spouse, teacher, etc. would not listen to you. How did it make you feel?

Prayer

Prayer is a wonderful gift, an open door of communication between God and His people. He encourages us to ask (Matthew 7:7–11). He hears (1 John 5:14), and He answers prayers (1 Chronicles 5:20).

We each pray in different ways, but when we are struggling we tend to go before God with a list of needs, worries, and suggestions. But what if we pray and things don't get better? We all know what it's like to pray and your loved one continue to get worse. Maybe finances get tighter, relatives get unreasonable, or caregivers don't show up.

> *The Lord is near. Do not be anxious about anything, but in every situation, by prayer and petition, with thanksgiving, present your requests to God. And the peace of God, which transcends all understanding, will guard your hearts and your minds in Christ Jesus.*
>
> —*PHILIPPIANS 4:5–7*

Instead of ranting at God, pushing Him harder for what you want, try this way of praying that calls upon the peaceful practices you've been exploring.

- Be aware of your situation and what you are feeling.
- Quiet your thoughts and feelings about the situation, and invite God to minister to you.
- Let go of expectations, and welcome what is happening.
- End in gratitude that His love and power are working in all for His good purposes, beyond what you can ask or imagine.

*What God arranges for us to experience at each moment is the best
and holiest thing that could happen to us.*

—JEAN-PIERRE DE CAUSSADE

Through regular practice, your flesh quiets, and the drama your ego tries to stir
up falls away as unnecessary, unimportant, and even unhelpful (filthy rags!).
Your list of needs becomes less important than hearing from God. He already
knows. You are now postured as a servant ready and willing to do what God has
created you to do. You are now praying in the Spirit!

*And pray in the Spirit on all occasions with all kinds of prayers and
requests. With this in mind, be alert and always keep on praying for
all the Lord's people.*

—EPHESIANS 6:18

Your whole view of the world will change from fear to connection because
you've tapped into an endless source of wisdom and peace. You may not be able
to understand how He is working, but you can have peace that He is working
what is best for all.

Prayer

*Father, peace seems within my reach now. Thank You for putting me on this
path of peace. Help me to stay on this path until peace defines me.*

Chapter 6
MAKING PEACE

Blessed are the peacemakers, for they will be called children of God.

—MATTHEW 5:9

There are two ways people tend to approach peace—by being a peacekeeper or a peacemaker. The average caregiver is a peacekeeper, working hard to keep everyone happy and comfortable and avoiding drama and upset at all costs (including the cost of their own physical and emotional health). Peacekeepers will limit their self-expression and allow internal pressure to build up instead of feeling safe to open up. The peacekeeper has not yet broken free from the tyranny of ego.

A peacemaker, on the other hand, actively pursues an environment where peace is possible—where all are welcomed, where no idea is squelched, where discomfort is embraced as a path to healing. The peacemaker is not threatened by opinions, conflict, and difficulties because she realizes the true, unshakable identity of herself and everyone else as beloved children of God. She knows that God is present, willing, and able to lead us to peace. There is great benefit in being a peacemaker.

Peacemakers who sow in peace reap a harvest of righteousness.

—JAMES 3:18

SCENARIO: Your loved one needs surgery. You've prayed with them and the family. You've given the control to God. But your loved one has the surgery and gets worse due to complications.

The peacekeeper might think she's helping everyone by carrying the guilt, taking responsibility for making the wrong decision. A scapegoat may offer false peace to a family looking for someone to blame—but overall the family is distanced from God and blame Him for not answering prayers.

The peacemaker might remind the family of the sovereignty of God, how His ways are not our ways, and how there's purpose and promises for times like these. She does not let the pain promote blame and division; instead she comforts the family in their grief and reminds them our Lord is familiar with sorrow (Isaiah 53:3). The peacemaker is rooted in her relationship with God and knows the truth of His promises. Because of that, she can make peace.

Describe a time when you could clearly see the difference between a peacekeeper and a peacemaker.

In these final chapters, we're going to explore the importance of and ways to make peace with God, ourselves, and others. The sad truth is many caregivers wander away from the One who can love and support them like no other. "Why did He let this happen? Where is God when I need Him the most?" Our own struggles and the suffering of the ones we care for drive us to the brink of shame, guilt, and unbelief. On top of that, our isolation has us alone with our thoughts, separated from a faith community. Reconciliation with God, self, and others is essential.

Peace with God

> *We are therefore Christ's ambassadors, as though God were*
> *making his appeal through us. We implore you on Christ's behalf:*
> *Be reconciled to God.*
>
> *—2 CORINTHIANS 5:20*

Not wanting a sovereign ruler, many prefer to search for peace through human activities and strivings, but the truth is there can be no peace without being able to trust in the love, plan, and purpose of an all-powerful, all-knowing God.

But we have a fickle relationship with Him. Because He's unseen and His ways are not our ways, it seems irresponsible, even ridiculous to fully rely on Him and not on our own understanding. Even when we decide we'll let His Holy Spirit run the show, we continue to wrestle with the questions of whether or not what we think we're hearing is indeed God's voice. The practice of quieting our ego and listening will take on even more importance in the light of these Scriptures.

Read Jeremiah 7:22–24 and Matthew 4:4. There are many more verses like these throughout the Bible. Why is it important for us to take the posture of a servant, willing to listen and hear our Lord?

God made us in His image, but we keep trying to make Him fit our ego-based imaginings of what He should be like so we can understand Him, even manipulate Him. But God is who He says He is whether you choose to believe it or not. The Truth of who you are and whose you are does not change just because you choose not to believe. We may have been through struggles, seen suffering, prayed prayers, and become frustrated with God that He won't cooperate. We may have shaken our fists at Him and walked away or, at the very least, we've doubted that He's real or that He Cares. But regardless of how you feel, He remains El Shaddai, God Almighty, Creator of Heaven and Earth.

Consider your true feelings toward God. Are you all in, completely surrendered, believing Him no matter what, or are you disappointed and doubting? Where are you on this scale? Circle the number.

10   9   8   7   6   5   4   3   2   1   0
All In   Doubting

*And without faith it is impossible to please God, because anyone who
comes to him must believe that he exists and that he rewards those
who earnestly seek him.*

—*HEBREWS 11:6*

If you circled anything but 10, you're having doubts about God. Search your
heart and list what causes you to doubt.

If you are ready to make peace with God in every area and be all in, pray like the
man in Mark 9:24, "I do believe; help me overcome my unbelief!"

The choice to believe is yours, but His Word tells us that we are His, here for
His purposes, doing His will through the power of His Spirit at work in us.
When we search for the meaning and purpose of our lives anywhere else but *in
Him*, we'll come up empty and frustrated every time.

*"For in him we live and move and have our being." As some of your
own poets have said, "We are his offspring."*

—*ACTS 17:28*

For he himself is our peace.

—*EPHESIANS 2:14*

From the moment we decided in the Garden that we didn't want to trust God but rather to know and make our own decisions, we've been building a world based on fear (envy, competition, judgment, anxiety, and hate). Just read the story of Cain and Abel in chapter four of Genesis. We're in the mess we're in because we think we know better than God. Isn't it time we make peace with God and let Him run His creation?

In particular, how would making peace with God help you as a caregiver?

Making peace with God isn't complicated or difficult. He made it easy. He's *already* at peace with you. You're forgiven with no condemnation, and the door to a loving relationship is already open. All you need to do is walk through.

Therefore, since we have been justified through faith, we have peace with God through our Lord Jesus Christ.

—*ROMANS 5:1*

Therefore, there is now no condemnation for those who are in Christ Jesus.

—*ROMANS 8:1*

Once you were alienated from God and were enemies in your minds
because of your evil behavior. But now he has reconciled you by
Christ's physical body through death to present you holy in his sight,
without blemish and free from accusation

—COLOSSIANS *1:21–22*

When you were dead in your sins and in the uncircumcision of your
flesh, God made you alive with Christ. He forgave us all our sins,
having canceled the charge of our legal indebtedness, which stood
against us and condemned us; he has taken it away, nailing it
to the cross.

—COLOSSIANS *2:13–14*

This is the essential message of the gospel, one that seems so hard for us to remember. God did it. We are *already* forgiven. We just need to accept that forgiveness for ourselves and then forgive others (Matthew 6:15; Luke 6:37). Like the prodigal son (Luke 15:11–32), all we have to do is go home. The Father is running to welcome us and celebrate our return.

Here are some simple steps you may take toward reconciliation with God:

Praise/Adoration/Worship: Worshipping God may come in the form of naming His attributes or proclaiming His status in the big picture of things. This will help you line up your thoughts in Truth. "You are in control of everything and everyone. You are good. You love us all. You forgive. You are all-powerful. Nothing and no one have authority over You—not disease, not disability, not even evil."

Confess: Admit that you have had wrong thinking and done wrong in certain areas. Confession helps clear the debris between you and God. "I keep thinking I'm in charge. I've said hurtful things to people I love. I've been angry with You, Lord, because You're not making things better. There are things I know I should do that I just don't want to do."

Thank: Gratitude is a great way to make peace with God. Thanking Him daily—for even the everyday things (food, running water, flowers, sunshine, etc.) reminds us who the source of everything is. "Lord, I am grateful for all that you have brought into my life, from the smallest touch of beauty in my daily life to the lifelong blessings that you have showered on me. Thank you for your mercy and your grace."

Prayer

Holy and Living God, I have experienced the crushing pressure of believing I am alone and in control. I now realize You are in control. I am willing to be yoked to You, to do this good work together with You so that when the work is done, I will know the exhilaration of hearing You say, "Well done, good and faithful servant!"

Chapter 7
PEACE WITH SELF

Brothers and sisters, think of what you were when you were called.
Not many of you were wise by human standards; not many were
influential; not many were of noble birth. But God chose the foolish
things of the world to shame the wise; God chose the weak things
of the world to shame the strong. God chose the lowly things of this
world and the despised things—and the things that are not—to
nullify the things that are, so that no one may boast before him.

—*1 CORINTHIANS 1:26–29*

There are very few people in this world who feel up to the tremendous task of caring for a person with exceptional needs. When you first learned that the care of this person would fall to you, how did you feel? Circle any that apply, and journal your thoughts on the following page.

- Why them? Why me?
- I don't have the patience.
- We don't have a good relationship.
- I'm too emotional.
- I have way too much on my plate.

Whether you were thrilled or angry, confused or prepared, it's probable there have been times when you've felt inadequate—emotionally and physically—or lacking the right resources—time, knowledge, or finances. You may question, "How did I get put in this position?"

The Truth is God has not made a mistake. You are chosen by God for this difficult but profound and beautiful work. You are chosen so that it will change you, bless (perhaps even heal) the people you're in relationship with, and benefit a world that has forgotten how to love and care for ourselves and each other.

When we disappoint or fail we tend to play the scene over and over in our minds and punish ourselves for our mistakes. Instead of learning from our mistakes and changing for the better, we're more likely to repeat the mistakes, condemned and believing that's just who we are. (i.e., I have a bad temper. I'm stubborn. I'm just not very smart. I'm not organized. I just don't have enough faith.)

Recalling our work from some of the first chapters, what are some of the labels you have put on yourself when it comes to your abilities as a caregiver?

I do not understand what I do. For what I want to do I do not do,
but what I hate I do.

—*ROMANS 7:15*

Get more context for what Paul is saying here, and read Romans 7:15–25. As Paul talks about doing what he doesn't want to do and not doing what he wants to do, we can relate! We know what's right and we want to do it, but we have a difficult time making the correct choices 100 percent of the time.

What do you keep doing that you don't want to do?

What have you not yet done that you want to do?

What if we could believe and trust that we are who God says we are? What if we believed the work we're doing is good and God chose the right person for the job? What if we could quiet old thoughts and let the Spirit guide us to wise and righteous decisions? What if you could be confident and fearless in difficult situations knowing that God will work it out? It's not up to you.

Consider some of the folks in the Bible who God used to do great things. Abraham, Moses, Peter, and Rahab were all flawed men and women who walked out their callings—one messy step at a time. They took wrong turns and seemed to encounter setbacks. Surely they felt inadequate at times, as though maybe God had picked the wrong person. But God still worked it all out for His purposes. You are in good company!

We feel arrogant or self-centered if we dare think of ourselves as beloved, chosen, created to do good, etc. Quite frankly it's easier for us to own the miserable sinner, failure, and unworthy labels. They give us excuses for our poor behavior and feed the lies of ego, but they also steal our peace.

My mind is a bad neighborhood that I try not to go into alone.

—*Anne Lamott*

Which comes easier for you—self-condemnation or self-confidence?

God's Word says that there is no condemnation for us (Romans 8:1), but ego relies on condemnation to keep feeding our frustration and pain. Jesus came to set us free and let us know we're forgiven and worthy of the Father's love. Until we receive that love and forgiveness for ourselves we won't be able to freely love and not condemn others. Condemnation is like the glue that holds the liar's labels on us. When condemnation dissolves in the power of forgiveness, the liar's labels slip off and we are left with our unchanging True self.

Loving yourself is not just an, "I'm okay. You're okay," kind of sentiment. Nor is it a way to indulge the ego. Quite the opposite. Loving yourself is an important part of self-care. It's recognizing and accepting you identity as His beloved child and forgiving yourself for all the lies you've been believing. It is the *most* important form of self-care. It's a commandment!

> *And the second is like it: "Love your neighbor as yourself."*
> —*MATTHEW 22:39*

The word *as* here is the Greek word *hos*, which can be translated, "in the same manner as, even as." This pertains well to two other teachings of Jesus. He tells us that we should do to others as we would have them do to us. And this makes so much sense when you accept His teaching that we are all part of one whole body. What you do to your brother you do to yourself *or* what you do to yourself you do to your brother.

When you accept your own belovedness, it's much easier to see the belovedness in others, including the person you care for, no matter how resistant, forgetful, unteachable, or even violent they may be. Until we learn to receive the forgiveness and grace that God extends to us, we'll struggle with extending it to others.

The people we care for need us to be able to extend unlimited forgiveness, grace, and patience. Imagine being bathed, fed, dressed, and ultimately managed by someone who's in pain (resentful, impatient, afraid) versus someone who's at peace, full of love, and able to extend tender mercy. Now take time to imagine the calming, healing impact your care might have if you were able to do it each day from love and peace. Put this book down and take time to let God reveal a new vision of care to you.

To receive forgiveness and grace you must first realize you need it. God is offering it, but we keep denying we need it. That's called pride. We can't live in peace if we're going to keep listening to and telling lies, making excuses, playing the victim—choosing to listen to ego over surrendering to the Spirit.

The good news is God has been relentlessly pursuing us, extending mercy, revealing His grace since that moment in the Garden when we chose poorly. (Read Genesis chapters 2 and 3).

- Even after He knew Adam and Eve were hiding in shame from Him, He went to them and called out, "Where are you?" (Genesis 3:9).

- Adam confessed his newfound fear of God because he'd been disobedient. Instead of wrath, God extended mercy to help Adam see the Truth. He asked, "Who told you that you were naked?" (v. 11). It wasn't the serpent. It wasn't God. We create our own guilt and shame when we listen to lies.
- Before sending them out of paradise, God made them garments of skin. He had to kill another creature to make those garments or "covering." Sin has a price. One day His own Son would make the final payment so that all who want to return may receive forgiveness and grace.

If God can forgive you, why can't you forgive yourself?

Here are some practical steps you can take toward making peace with yourself:

At any given time, we're all doing the best we can. Like Paul we may know better, but we just haven't developed the skills to get it right 100 percent of the time. Instead of beating yourself up or going down the same wrong path again, pause, be still, listen, and give yourself a chance to respond from your true self, the you that is always at peace and in Christ.

Stop worrying about what people think. Most of the time they're not thinking what you think they're thinking. That's your own self-depreciating ego! When someone gives you their opinion, if it's Truth, thank them and consider the message. If it's not Truth, be kind and thank them anyway, then bless the messenger.

Look for the good in yourself and acknowledge it. When doing the hard work of caregiving, say to yourself, "That was hard, but I did it!" Even if you wanted to scream and didn't, congratulate yourself for practicing patience. You're recognizing that you have choices, and you're choosing new and better ways.

As caregivers we spend a lot of time separated from the rest of the world—with people who are nonverbal or uncommunicative, in a medical haze of doctors, nurses, therapists, waiting in pharmacies, offices and hospitals, exhausted at the bedside of someone who is suffering.

> *As a prisoner for the Lord, then, I urge you to live a life worthy of the calling you have received. Be completely humble and gentle; be patient, bearing with one another in love. Make every effort to keep the unity of the Spirit through the bond of peace.*
>
> —*EPHESIANS 4:1–3*

We can feel isolated, and isolation can feel like prison if we're afraid to be alone with our thoughts. But with the Spirit, what seems to be isolation can become solitude: a place to be still, listen, reconnect with Truth, and find peace.

> *Solitude is the garden for our hearts, which yearn for love. It is the place where our aloneness can bear fruit. It is the home for our restless bodies and anxious minds. Solitude, whether it is connected with a physical space or not, is essential for our spiritual lives. It is not an easy place to be, since we are so insecure and fearful that we are easily distracted by whatever promises immediate satisfaction. Solitude is not immediately satisfying, because in solitude we meet our demons, our addictions, our feelings of lust and anger, and our immense need for recognition and approval. But if we do not run away, we will meet there also the One who says, "Do not be afraid. I am with you, and I will guide you through the valley of darkness."*
>
> —**HENRI NOUWEN,** *BREAD FOR THE JOURNEY*

Tired and afraid, we pick up the phone, turn on the TV, take a pill to make us sleep—anything to not listen to our own toxic thoughts. But now we have a new choice. We can quiet our thoughts. We can listen for the Shepherd who will lead us beside still waters and make us lie down in green pastures. And there, in a state of rest and trust with our Shepherd, He will restore our souls (Psalm 23).

Prayer

Lord, I confess I have been tough on myself and taken it out on others. Bless me to realize the Truth of who I am, a beloved child of God, and forgive myself (no more condemnation) and live from peace.

Chapter 8
PEACE WITH OTHERS

Let the peace of Christ rule in your hearts, since as members of one body you were called to peace. And be thankful.

—COLOSSIANS 3:15

People can be our greatest sources of conflict, competition, resentment, jealousy, bitterness, and anger. And just like Adam and Eve did, we're willing to blame others. They blamed the snake. We blame politicians, neighbors, terrorists, grade school bullies, etc. for our discontent and pain. If these people are the reason we're upset, we're doomed to a life of no peace. They're not all going to realize their flaws, change, and apologize.

With whom are you currently experiencing challenging differences?

Through His death on the Cross, Christ has destroyed the barriers between us and others so we can have unity with people who are not like us. We are all being drawn together to become a holy and living temple, a dwelling in which God lives by His Spirit (Ephesians 2:14–22).

We're created to be unique, different. This may seem like a cruel joke on God's part, but it's actually essential to a very beautiful plan. Like the soil, rain, and sun freely give themselves for the growth and life of the seed, so we are each uniquely gifted to freely give ourselves for the growth and life of others.

A goal of this study is to realize that we're an essential part of a whole—not excluded but necessary. This is true for you, the person you care for, your enemies, the folks who drive you nuts. Everyone belongs, even the difficult ones. Once you discover the divine in yourself, you can more easily recognize it in others.

Consider this image of the body of Christ on page 73.

We're created as part of a whole, a fellowship of believers. Take a moment to read 1 Corinthians 12:4—13:13. We're one large organism (John 17:22) held together by love. We are the particles, and God is the energy—love—between the particles.

We have been uniquely gifted to serve each other (1 Peter 4:10), to carry each other's burdens (Galatians 6:2). We're so closely interconnected as part of His body that what you do to another you're also doing to yourself (Luke 6:31) and to Him (Matthew 25:40).

So in Christ we, though many, form one body, and each member belongs to all the others.

—ROMANS 12:5

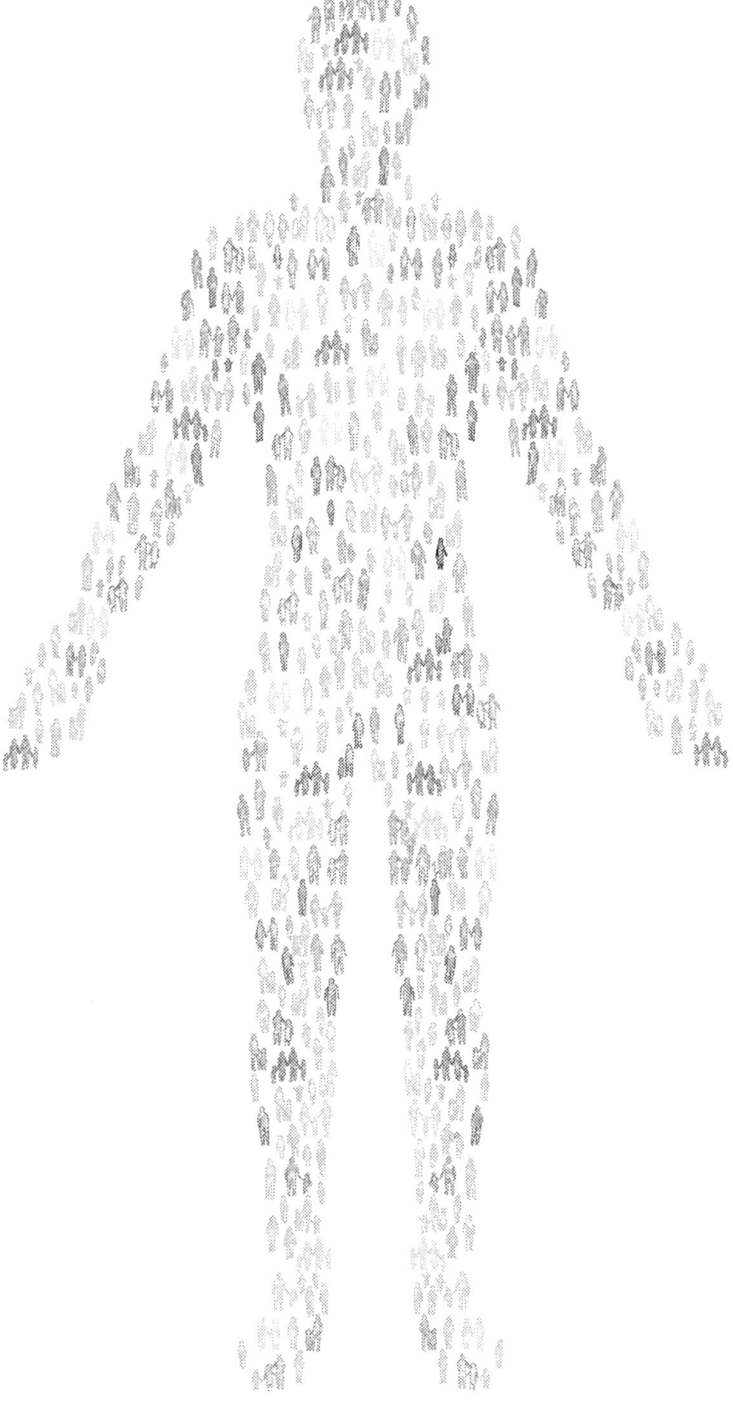

Not everyone will see things as you do, feel what you feel, or think what you think. It's your belief that they *should* be able to see, feel, and think the way you do that's causing you pain. But under the anger, frustration, even rage—there is a longing for reunion.

Return to the image of the body of Christ. Find the area where the eyes would be and circle it. Now find the area where the toes are and circle it. The eyes are made of cells that keep them moist and supple. The toes have toenails made of cells to keep them hard. They're both part of the whole body. Though far apart from each other on the body, both are important to the body as a whole.

How ridiculous would it be for the toenail to judge the eyeball wrongly for being soft? The toenail may not realize it, but the eye helps keep the body from stumping the toe! (Recall 1 Corinthians 12:21–26.) Only God knows what's best for the whole body and all its many wonderful parts.

We judge others who are not like us to be *other* and tend to blame them when things go wrong. You may fantasize about the peace of not having to deal with people who are not like you, but God says we *belong* to each other. We are to build community and work toward peace and mutual edification (Romans 14:19). Think about it. A rogue cell in the body is one that tries to function on its own terms and no longer functions for the benefit of the body. In doing so, it destroys other cells. We call this *cancer*.

> *A new command I give you: Love one another. As I have loved*
> *you, so you must love one another. By this everyone will know that*
> *you are my disciples, if you love one another.*
>
> —JOHN 13:34–35

Loving people whose opinions and preferences are different from yours can be difficult. One of the greatest enemies of love is letting ourselves get offended, allowing our feelings to get hurt, and then carrying a grudge.

Perhaps you've been in conflict with the person for whom you are caring. Maybe you've been hurt by a friend or relative who thinks your care is inadequate, a doctor with no bedside manner, a demanding boss who doesn't understand, or a church that's turned a blind eye. Trying to work with people, let alone love them when you feel offended, can be toxic for everyone, but if you're waiting for them to realize their flaws, change, and apologize, there may never be peace.

Jesus modeled forgiveness, surrender, even service to those who thwart us. He never encouraged retaliation, nor did He demand retribution. His behavior was shocking as He stood silent in the face of His accosters, mockers, and accusers. God's Lamb surrendered in silence to the Cross (Isaiah 53:7; Matthew 26:62–63).

It's not wrong to be upset (read how Jesus became angry with the money changers in Mark 11:15), especially with injustice or violence, but getting offended doesn't change things. It only adds to the problem. We've been letting ourselves be offended by people who are not like us forever, and where has it gotten us? If we want to change things and find a way to make peace with others, we must quiet our ego, listen, and then take the next steps in peace under the guidance of His Holy Spirit. That's how positive, righteous change happens.

How might you love and make peace with others who are different from you, even against you? Here are a few suggestions.

Forgiveness (Matthew 6:12–14; 18:21–22) is probably the first thing that comes to mind, and that is the most essential. But the context is important. Are you forgiving someone for being who they are or for the pain they triggered in you?

Forgiving someone for who they are implies judgment. "Bless your heart. I'll forgive you because you don't know any better." Forgiving someone for triggering pain in you calls for humility, "I can forgive you because *I* don't know better. I haven't yet come to terms with my own wounds and weaknesses." Remember peace is your choice, regardless of circumstances.

Acceptance (Matthew 7:1–5; Acts 10:34; Romans 14:1–4) can be tough for many Christians. Many of us were taught to be moral and behavioral police. But who are we to judge or condemn when not one of us is perfect (Matthew 12:7; John 8:10–11)? Who are we to judge someone else's servant? God is pursuing them just as He is pursuing you. Luke 6:37 says, "Do not judge, and you will not be judged. Do not condemn, and you will not be condemned. Forgive, and you will be forgiven."

If we are to help the Lord evangelize the world, let us do it His way. Let us welcome people as they are (tax collector, prostitute, Pharisee, prison guard, rich young ruler) and reveal to them the truth of who they are in Christ—beloved children of God, your brother or sister.

Compassion is one of our most powerful tools (Philippians 2:1–4). We know what it's like to hurt, and if we have come to terms with our own wounds, weaknesses, and needs, we can help others with theirs.

Unfortunately the essence of compassion has been corrupted. We've been taught that compassion is helping those less fortunate than ourselves. That's actually toxic charity when we believe we have power that others don't and that they need us. The only one who anyone needs is God. Jesus revealed that principle over and over again. We "enter in" with those who are suffering, and from that common ground we invite *God* to meet our needs.

Jesus also tells us to give to others what we think we need. That makes sense when considered in the context that we are all connected. As Luke 6:31 and 38 say, "Do to others as you would have them do to you. . . . Give, and it will be given to you. A good measure, pressed down, shaken together and running over, will be poured into your lap. For with the measure you use, it will be measured to you."

Here's an illustration that may help you understand compassion. Let's pretend we're walking down a road with someone and they suddenly fall down a hole.

We can simply not notice and keep walking. That's oblivion.

We can notice and keep walking. That's apathy.

We can notice, then sit at the top of the hole telling them about the time we fell down the hole (hoping that will help). That's sympathy.

We can jump down the hole and be with them in their pain. That's empathy.

Or we can jump down the hole with the ladder that will get us both out. That's compassion.

This is where it becomes evident that if we're going to be able to love and serve others, we have to have done the heart work, the inner healing, of receiving the love and forgiveness of God so that we can extend it (the ladder) to others.

We were created for connection and community with God and others in Christ. Caring is an essential part of our oneness—not only the care we give to the one with exceptional needs, our family, and our friends, but also to all who cross our path (consider the parable of the good Samaritan found in Luke 10:29–37). You may think that's impossible, but when you learn to drink deeply from The Well, you will discover unlimited abundance. You don't have to take everyone in to live with you, but you will find you have enough to give—a hug, a kind word, a listening ear, a plate of supper. It is then we will become the church Jesus designed—people taking care of people.

Do nothing out of selfish ambition or vain conceit. Rather, in humility value others above yourselves, not looking to your own interests but each of you to the interests of the others.

—*Philippians 2:3–4*

Prayer

Lord, I've allowed myself to become offended by my brothers and sisters. I've held grudges and swore I'd never forgive or forget. I now see why Jesus tells us to forgive. I'm hurting myself and grieving Your Holy Spirit. I may not be able to forget, but Lord, please help me to forgive so that I may be a source of healing and experience peace.

Chapter 9
PEACE WITH TIME AND TRANSITION

I have given them your word and the world has hated them, for they are not of the world any more than I am of the world. My prayer is not that you take them out of the world but that you protect them from the evil one. They are not of the world, even as I am not of it. Sanctify them by the truth; your word is truth. As you sent me into the world, I have sent them into the world.

—JOHN 17:14–18

When we decide to live our True Self, from our divine nature (2 Peter 1:4), and let the Holy Spirit guide us to live out God's purposes for our lives, we are realizing the truth of John 17:14–18. In a nutshell, we've realized who we are and whose we are—spiritual beings, not of this world, but sent into it on a divine assignment.

What a beautiful moment of revelation and realization! Yet it leaves us in a uniquely difficult state of being. We become strangers to this world. We find ourselves standing in a gap between Spirit and flesh, heaven and earth, eternal and temporal. This can be a source of internal conflict. We need the conviction to let our minds be renewed (choose truth, choose Spirit, choose life) and no longer conform to the pattern of this world (Romans 12:2).

What is the pattern of this world? We've explored bits and pieces of it in previous chapters—what the world dictates as important, beautiful, worthy, essential, etc. In this chapter we'll look at two elements in the pattern of this world that are particularly stressful for caregivers—time and transition from this world to the next.

Time

> *But do not forget this one thing, dear friends: With the Lord a day is like a thousand years, and a thousand years are like a day.*
>
> —*2 PETER 3:8*

Time in the kingdom of God is different from earthly time. Yes, He created day and night and set the sun, moon, and stars in the heavens, but God's kingdom functions in the eternal while we on earth seem trapped in linear, temporal time.

Ancient civilizations developed devices and calendars to be able to prepare for seasons of feast and famine, planting crops, and predicting seasonal phenomena (floods, fires, storms), etc.

But the ego has turned time into a world system to be monetized (i.e., hourly wages) and dictate limitations (i.e., "Time's up!" or "You're too old."). We are acutely aware that our time will come to an end.

This perspective of time pushes and rushes us to get as much out of this life as possible. Rest and trust (Isaiah 30:15) seem impossible in a world that's screaming, "Hurry up!" There just never seems to be enough time, and when you're caring for someone else, the stress and pressure of time seems to increase. Here are a few thoughts specific to caregivers that create excessive pressure around time.

- Time for what you had planned seems to have been stolen from you.
- You're adding another person's schedule on top of your own.
- You both long for the time before there was a disease or disability.
- This time of sickness or disability almost seems not to "count."
- The person you're caring for moves slowly.
- You are more aware of the inevitability of time running out.
- Is caregiving worth your time?
- We can't wait. We want healing/relief *now*.

What are some aspects of time that burden you or steal your peace?

Here are some simple suggestions that may help you make peace with time.

Planning: Some people think that making peace with time is all about managing it better. But when caring for people with intellectual and physical disabilities, chronic illness, and cognitive decline, that can be a futile exercise. A sitter who doesn't show up, a jammed waiting room, an emotional meltdown, etc. can blow our carefully planned schedule in an instant.

Instead keep your plans relaxed, and be prepared to change plans on a moment's notice. It may not be any easier, but you are more in control and can remain calm and centered as you put Plan B into action.

Accepting *flexible* as your new normal can prepare others that you might not be able to fulfill mutual obligations. We create stress and agitation for everyone when we try and make our loved one conform to the patterns of this world. It's okay to ask for grace. You create an atmosphere of understanding instead of offense.

Presence: If we consider caregiving a burden, a problem, a source of pain, we may try not to focus on it or truly engage with the experience. We can make ourselves miserable simply by finding it impossible to accept life just as it is thereby making an enemy of the present moment—creating stress. You may be using the present only as a means to get to the future where you hope to find relief, comfort, contentment, fulfillment, etc. But those qualities only exist in the present. You can't actually be content yesterday or tomorrow. You can remember being content. You can hope to be content, but you can't actually be content any time but right now, in the present. Perhaps that's what Paul meant when he said, "I tell you, now is the time of God's favor, now is the day of salvation" (2 Corinthians 6:2).

The present moment is where love, peace, joy, creativity, and contentment dwell. We may regret the past or make plans for the future, but at any given moment, now is all we actually have (Luke 12:16–20; James 4:13–17). What you are looking for, what you need *already* exists. It's available *now*, but it eludes you because you are not aware or watchful in the present moment.

Perseverance: Many consider their caregiving years as time to be endured, coped with, but loving care is what we're here to do for each other. So instead of expending negative energy trying to figure out how to get out of caregiving or focusing on the day it may end, maintain an attitude of perseverance. God is doing a good work. It may be difficult work, but it is good, and you will commit to learning and growing through the experience. Let perseverance finish its work so that you may be mature and complete, not lacking anything, that you may have peace (James 1:4).

Patience: It is one thing to persevere, to stick with it, to not avoid the tough stuff, but it is quite another thing to be able to do it with peace. That is patience. Hope is implied in patience. That there is a reward we are waiting for (Habakkuk 2:3; Luke 21:19). That each moment is an essential part of a process. Time takes on a new meaning when we know we are waiting for something wonderful that will surely come.

Perspective: Aligning with God's Truth about time can offer us peace.

Time is a good gift created by God for us (Genesis 1:14).

God created us for His plans and purposes (Proverbs 19:21).

He's given us time to fulfill those purposes and be satisfied (Ecclesiastes 3:13).

He even marked out the appointed time in history that He would have us do this work (Acts 17:26).

While He has allowed us to know time through seasons and cycles, we don't necessarily know God's timing of events (Ecclesiastes 3:11; Acts 1:7)—when someone will die, when healing will occur, when finances will run out, etc.

He has given us life in all its fullness, no matter how long or short ours might be (John 10:10).

Fullness and busyness are not the same. Love is what makes life full, not experiences and accomplishments (1 Corinthians 13:1–13).

Time for rest is mandatory (Leviticus 23:32).

The value of our time on earth will be revealed in eternity (2 Corinthians 4:16).

Transition

Therefore we do not lose heart. Though outwardly we are wasting away, yet inwardly we are being renewed day by day. For our light and momentary troubles are achieving for us an eternal glory that far outweighs them all. So we fix our eyes not on what is seen, but on what is unseen, since what is seen is temporary, but what is unseen is eternal.

—2 CORINTHIANS 4:16–18

Second Corinthians 4:16–18 gives such a beautiful picture of how simple and marvelous the transition from this world to the next must be—like an ice cube melting into a glass of water. As this body (and ego) diminishes, we lose our sense of separation from the Greater Whole. We realize more fully our eternal True Self, our belonging in Christ.

This passage also reveals that the troubles of this world have had purpose, giving us choice to overcome the world and chose the truth of who we are. So shift your gaze now from this world and all that steals our peace to the unshakable peace of the kingdom of God.

The ego fears the end of the physical. We have built a multimillion-dollar antiaging industry on that fear. We've created a culture where you must remain fast, strong, smart, and productive, or you'll be culled out of the herd.

There are few remaining cultures that treat the sick, disabled, elderly, and dying as highly honored and important members of the community, full of wisdom and close to God. Yet Paul tells us the weak are indispensable parts of the whole (1 Corinthians 12:22). They have much to teach us.

Discovering true ID—yours and theirs: Being with those who have come to an acceptance in death, having let go of their earthly power—money, looks, status, intelligence, etc.—can help *us* on our journey of inner renewal and healing, teaching us how to trust and stop clinging to anything but God as our sole security and identity.

Living by the Spirit: Those who are nearing death have nothing more to prove. They have nothing to lose. It's far easier to surrender to the Spirit. They have truly put off the old self to put on the new (Ephesians 4:22–24). It's ironic, but when we're ready to die, we are finally ready to live!

Practicing peace: Spending quiet time (no words, no work) just being with someone who has accepted death is an incredibly holy time. In the stillness of just being members of the body of Christ (not individuals), divine connection and presence becomes palpable. "For where two or three gather in my name, there am I with them" (Matthew 18:20).

These Scripture passages may offer peace to you and your family around the subject of death.

But I will see Your face in righteousness; when I awake, I will be satisfied with Your presence.

—Psalm 17:15 HCSB

Though you have made me see troubles, many and bitter, you will restore my life again; from the depths of the earth you will again bring me up. You will increase my honor and comfort me once more.

—PSALM *71:20–21*

I give them eternal life, and they shall never perish; no one will snatch them out of my hand.

—JOHN *10:28*

For none of us lives for ourselves alone, and none of us dies for ourselves alone. If we live, we live for the Lord; and if we die, we die for the Lord. So, whether we live or die, we belong to the Lord.

—ROMANS *14:7–8*

However, as it is written: "What no eye has seen, what no ear has heard, and what no human mind has conceived"—the things God has prepared for those who love him.

—1 CORINTHIANS *2:9*

Because we know that the one who raised the Lord Jesus from the dead will also raise us with Jesus and present us with you to himself.

—2 CORINTHIANS *4:14*

I eagerly expect and hope that I will in no way be ashamed but will have sufficient courage so that now as always Christ will be exalted in my body, whether by life or by death. For to me, to live is Christ and to die is gain. If I am to go on living in the body, this will mean fruitful labor for me. Yet what shall I choose? I do not know!

—PHILIPPIANS *1:20–22*

There have been saints, prophets, teachers, mystics—humans who have glimpsed the Truth. They can teach us about their own spiritual journeys, but there is only one who has come from Truth in perfection to show The Way for us all (John 14:6; Matthew 22:16). Of the many other teachers, Jesus is the only one with an empty tomb. He is alive and functioning in His divine authority (Ephesians 1:20; Colossians 3:1; Hebrews 8:1–2) with a place prepared for us to join Him (John 14:2).

> *Jesus answered, "Even if I testify on my own behalf, my testimony is valid, for I know where I came from and where I am going.*
>
> *—JOHN 8:14*

> *Jesus knew that the Father had put all things under his power, and that he had come from God and was returning to God.*
>
> *—JOHN 13:3*

> *I came from the Father and entered the world; now I am leaving the world and going back to the Father.*
>
> *—JOHN 16:28*

> *What does "he ascended" mean except that he also descended to the lower, earthly regions?*
>
> *—EPHESIANS 4:9*

Jesus is the author of our peace. His assignment is to wake us up to the truth of our belonging through the forgiveness of the Cross and remind us of our divine assignment to do the same for others. Read John 17 and be strengthened anew with this beautiful prayer of Jesus for you and me.

For in him we live and move and have our being.

—*ACTS 17:28*

Never will I leave you; never will I forsake you.

—*HEBREWS 13:5*

This is how we know that we live in him and he in us: He has given us of his Spirit.

—*1 JOHN 4:13*

As we come to know Him more, we can trust Him more. He is not just waiting for us on the other side. He is here now—guiding, teaching, loving through the power of His Holy Spirit. He *cannot* abandon us. We will forever dwell in Him and He in us. And so we have peace.

When we are at peace, we find the freedom to be most fully who we are, even in the worst of times. We let go of what is nonessential and embrace what is essential. We empty ourselves so that God may more fully work within us. And we become instruments in the hands of the Lord.

—JOSEPH CARDINAL BERNARDIN, *THE GIFT OF PEACE*

Prayer

God of Peace, bless me to love and serve You and others from love and peace all my days.

Notes

1. "Evercare Study of Caregivers in Decline: A Close-Up Look at the Health Risks of Caring for a Loved One," Evercare, in collaboration with National Alliance for Caregiving, September 2006, https://www.caregiving.org/data/Caregivers%20in%20Decline%20Study-FINAL-lowres.pdf.

2. Family Caregiver Alliance, Caregiver Assessment: Voices and Views from the Field. Report from a National Consensus Development Conference, vol. II. (San Francisco: Author, 2006), 14–15.

3. "Caregiver Health," Family Caregiver Alliance National Center on Caregiving, accessed August 15, 2019, https://www.caregiver.org/caregiver-health.

If you enjoyed this book, will you consider sharing the message with others?

Let us know your thoughts at info@ironstreammedia.com. You can also let the author know by visiting or sharing a photo of the cover on our social media pages or leaving a review at a retailer's site. All of it helps us get the message out!

Facebook.com/IronStreamMedia

Ascender Books is an imprint of Iron Stream Media, which derives its name from Proverbs 27:17, "As iron sharpens iron, so one person sharpens another."

This sharpening describes the process of discipleship, one to another. With this in mind, Iron Stream Media provides a variety of solutions for churches, ministry leaders, and nonprofits ranging from in-depth Bible study curriculum and Christian book publishing to custom publishing and consultative services. Through our popular Life Bible Study, Student Life Bible Study brands, and New Hope imprints, ISM provides web-based full-year and short-term Bible study teaching plans as well as printed devotionals, Bibles, and discipleship curriculum.

For more information on ISM and Ascender Books, please visit

IronStreamMedia.com

Printed in the United States
By Bookmasters